How Things Grow

From Kitten

to Cat

Sally Morgan

Belitha Press

First published in the UK in 2002 by
Belitha Press
A member of **Chrysalis** Books plc
64 Brewery Road, London N7 9NT

ISBN 1 84138 372 4

British Library Cataloguing in Publication Data
for this book is available from the British Library.

Series editor: Jean Coppendale
Designer: Angie Allison
Picture researchers: Sally Morgan and Terry Forshaw
Consultant: Bethan Currenti

Printed in Hong Kong

10 9 8 7 6 5 4 3 2 1

Picture acknowledgements:
All photography Chrysalis Images/Robert Pickett with the exception of:
4 Papilio/Robert Pickett; 5, front cover (inset) & 28 (BR) Papilio/Melvyn Lawes; 6, 11,
19 & front cover (inset), 20 & back cover (L), 21 Warren Photographic/Jane Burton;
25 RSPCA Photolibrary/Angela Hampton; 26 Papilio; 27 Ecoscene/Neeraj Mishra.

Contents

What is a cat?

The cat is a type of animal called
a **mammal**. Its body is covered in hairs.
Cats give birth to young called kittens.
The kittens feed on their mother's milk
for the first weeks of their lives.

A cat can run,
jump and climb. It can
jump distances many times
the length of its own body.

This young cat is watching a ball. It has excellent senses of sight and smell.

Cats are **carnivores**. This means that they eat meat. They hunt and kill other animals for food. Pet cats are related to wild cats such as lions, tigers and leopards.

A kitten is born

The kittens are born one by one.

Just before the kittens are born, the mother cat finds a safe place to make her nest. She gives birth to a **litter** of five or six kittens. As soon as each kitten is born, the mother licks it clean.

When all the kittens have been born,
they have their first drink of milk.
The kittens' eyes are shut and they cannot
hear anything. The first thing they do is
crawl towards their mother's warm body.

The kittens
quickly learn to drink
their mother's milk.

The first week

The kittens spend all day drinking their mother's milk and sleeping. They stay close to each other to keep warm. Their eyes are still shut, so they use their senses of smell and touch to find their way around.

The kittens curl up together to stay warm.

The kittens learn to suck on their mother's **nipples** to get milk.

When they are hungry the kittens crawl towards the smell of their mother's milk. After the kittens have fed, the mother cat licks them clean, using her rough tongue..

The mother cat licks all of her kittens clean.

9

Exploring

When the kitten is about 10 days old its eyes open and it can see for the first time.

The kittens are nearly two weeks old and they are growing quickly. They are interested in what is around them. They can hear now and they soon learn to move their head around to follow noises.

The kittens can also make sounds. They can purr when they are happy and hiss when they are angry. They can stand up now and they are starting to explore. Their mother watches them and if a kitten crawls too far she picks it up and carries it back to the nest.

The kitten is taken back to its safe nest.

A change of food

For the first month, the mother cat feeds her kittens milk. She has to eat extra food to make sure she has enough milk for them.

The kitten's first teeth are small but very sharp.

These kittens are trying solid food for the first time.

When the kittens' teeth appear they are ready to be **weaned**. This means that they change from drinking milk to eating solid food. Each day, the kittens eat more of their solid food and less milk.

Play time

Kittens tumble about but they do not hurt each other.

The kittens spend the day playing and sleeping. They love playing with each other but they get tired quickly. They sleep for many hours, huddled together.

Play is important. The kittens chase balls and play with toys. Playing helps them to learn how to hunt. If the kittens play too roughly or they hurt their mother, she tells them off.

Kittens learn to watch and catch when they play with their toys.

Learning to hunt

Cats have sharp claws
to help them catch their food.
They also have sharp teeth.
Their front teeth are for biting.
The larger teeth at the back of
their mouths are for crushing food.

Kittens learn to **pounce** on moving toys. When they are older they will pounce on small animals such as mice.

Kittens have to learn to hunt so they can catch food. Cats catch animals by creeping up on them. They have to move very slowly so that they are not spotted. Kittens learn to hunt by watching their mother.

A kitten keeps its claws sharp by scratching them on a special pole covered in rope.

Leaving home

Kittens grow quickly. By the time a kitten is ten weeks old it can feed and look after itself. It is ready to leave its mother and go to a new home.

This kitten is eight weeks old. Soon it will leave its mother.

The kitten slowly **explores** its
new home. It sniffs everything
to get used to the new smells.

When a kitten
arrives at its new home it may feel
worried and lonely. It has to get
used to living on its own. It will
miss its brothers and sisters.

Watching cats

You can learn a lot about cats by watching them. When a cat rushes up to greet you it rubs itself against your leg. It is rubbing its **scent** all over your leg. When a cat is happy it purrs. Its ears are forward and its tail is lifted up.

You can learn a lot about cats when you play with them. You can watch for the signs that tell you if the cat is happy or angry.

20

This is an angry cat.
Its back is arched up
and its fur is on end.
The cat is warning you
that it will attack.

Cats keep themselves
clean by licking their
fur. Their rough
tongues take away
all the dirt.

An angry cat
will growl or hiss. It
arches its back and
puffs out its fur so
that it looks bigger.
Its tail swishes from
side to side.

Finding a mate

A cat is fully grown by the time it is six months old. Female cats are ready to have kittens when they are about one year old. Most cats give birth to kittens during the spring and summer months.

By the time a cat is one year old she is ready to have kittens.

This cat is pregnant. Her body is large and she eats a lot of food.

A cat is **pregnant** for nine weeks. The kittens grow inside her body. By the seventh week, you can see the kittens moving around inside her body when she lies down. She needs to eat a lot of food to feed her unborn kittens.

Getting old

This old cat is sleeping in the sun.

Cats can live for up to 20 years.
The oldest cat in the world was called
Ma and she was 34 years old. When
cats get old, they spend much of
the day asleep.

Older cats may get fat as they do not run around and climb as much as they did when they were younger. Sometimes their teeth fall out and they find it difficult to eat their food. Some cats have skin problems and their hair becomes thin.

An older cat may become ill and need to be taken to the vet.

The cat family

Lions live on the grasslands of Africa. This group of lionesses and cubs is called a pride. The lionesses hunt together.

Pet cats are related to wild cats. The biggest cats are the lions and tigers. Lions live together in a group called a **pride**. The female lion is called lioness and it is the lionesses that do the hunting.

Tigers live on their own and they hunt in the forest. Cheetahs and leopards also live alone. Cheetahs use their great speed to catch their prey.

The leopard lives and hunts alone. It rests in the branches of trees during the day.

The life cycle

1 A new born kitten is deaf and its eyes are shut.

2 The kitten spends its first week drinking and sleeping. It finds its way around by smell and touch.

8 When a female cat is one year old she is ready to have kittens.

7 The cat is fully grown after six months.

3 After 10 days the kitten's eyes open and it can explore its surroundings.

4 The kitten's teeth appear after three weeks. They are small, but very sharp.

6 After ten weeks, the kitten is old enough to look after itself. It can leave its mother and go to a new home.

5 By the time the kitten is four weeks old, it is ready to start eating solid food.

Glossary

carnivores   Animals that eat meat. Cats, dogs, bears and weasels are all carnivores.

explores   Makes a very careful search of an area.

litter   All the babies born at one time to a cat or dog.

mammal   A type of animal with fur which feeds its young with its own milk.

nipples Small lumps on the chest of the mother cat from which the kittens suck milk.

pounce   To jump down suddenly on to something.

pregnant   Having unborn kittens developing inside the mother's body.

pride   A group of lions.

scent   The smell of something.

weaned   Moved from a diet of milk to a diet of solid food.

index